Happiness Always

Happiness Always

MQP

Happiness seems
made to be shared.

Jean Racine

Success is not the key to happiness. Happiness is the key to success. If you love what you are doing, you will be successful.

Herman Cain

Only the soul that
loves is happy.

Johann Wolfgang von Goethe

That's the difference between me and the rest of the world! Happiness isn't good enough for me! I demand euphoria!

Jean Calvin

Happiness is the spiritual experience of living every minute with love, grace and gratitude.

Denis Waitley

Life is to be fortified by
many friendships. To love
and be loved is the greatest
happiness of existence.

Sydney Smith

Happiness is a sort of atmosphere you can live in sometimes when you're lucky. Joy is a light that fills you with hope and faith and love.

Adela Rogers St. Johns

All who would win joy,
must share it; happiness
was born a twin.

Lord Byron

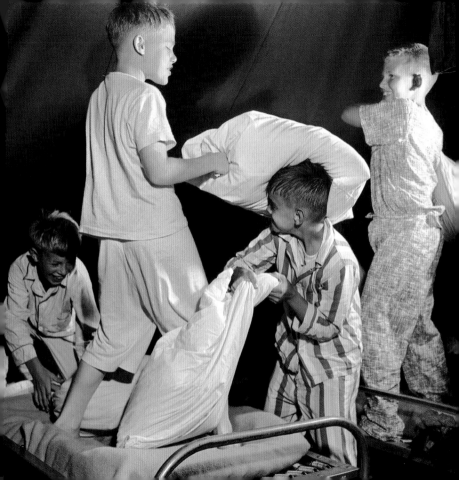

Present mirth hath present laughter.

William Shakespeare

Happiness is a set
of new clubs and a
round with a set of
old friends.

Miff McCluskey

Animals love happiness
almost as much as we do.

Sidonie-Gabrielle Colette

There are as many kinds of
beauty as there are habitual
ways of seeking happiness.

Charles Baudelaire

Men of the noblest
dispositions think
themselves happiest
when others share their
happiness with them.

Barry Duncan

Universal happiness keeps the wheels steadily turning.

Aldous Huxley

The greatest happiness of life is the conviction that we are loved—loved for ourselves, or rather, loved in spite of ourselves.

Victor Hugo

Happiness does not consist in things themselves but in the relish we have of them.

François, duc de La Rochefoucauld

It is by studying little things that we attain the great art of having as little misery and as much happiness as possible.

Samuel Johnson

Knowledge is happiness, because to have knowledge—broad, deep knowledge—is to know true ends from false, and lofty things from low.

Helen Keller

Cheerfulness is a
policy; happiness
is a talent.

Mason Cooley

41

Poetry is the record of the best and happiest moments of the happiest and best minds.

Percy Bysshe Shelley

Beauty for some provides escape,
Who gain happiness in eyeing
The gorgeous buttocks of the ape.

Aldous Huxley

My whole working philosophy is that the only stable happiness for mankind is that it shall live married in blessed union to womankind—intimacy, physical and psychical between a man and a wife.

D. H. Lawrence

Happiness walks on busy feet.

Kitte Turmell

A good cook is like a sorceress
who dispenses happiness.

Elsa Schiaparelli

A mother's happiness
is like a beacon,
lighting up the future
but reflected also on
the past in the guise
of fond memories.

Honoré de Balzac

Never fear spoiling
children by making them
too happy. Happiness is
the atmosphere in which
all good affections grow.

Thomas Bray

All happiness depends
on a leisurely breakfast.

John Gunther

The moments of happiness we enjoy take us by surprise. It is not that we seize them, but that they seize us.

Ashley Montagu

In life, as in cricket,
happiness comes from
playing a straight bat.

Dharminder Kang

Wheresoever you go, go with all your heart.

Confucius

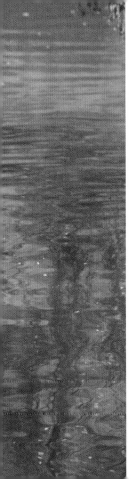

We seek happiness in boats and carriage rides.

Horace

The secret of
happiness is to
make others
believe they are
the cause of it.

Al Batt

True happiness consists not in the multitude of friends, but in the worth and choice.

Ben Jonson

Happiness is the
only good and the
way to be happy is
to make others so.

Robert Green Ingersoll

It is neither wealth
nor splendor, but
tranquillity and
occupation which
give happiness.

Thomas Jefferson

Happiness does not notice
the passing of time.

Chinese proverb

It enhances our sense of the grand security and serenity of nature, to observe the still undisturbed economy and content of the fishes of this century, their happiness a regular fruit of the summer.

Henry David Thoreau

Happiness: a good
bank account, a
good cook, and a
great digestion.

Jean-Jacques Rousseau

The foolish man
seeks happiness in
the distance, the wise
grows it under his feet.

James Oppenheim

Every gift from a
friend is a wish for
your happiness.

Richard Bach

Happiness comes of the capacity to feel deeply, to enjoy simply, to think freely, to risk life, to be needed.

Storm Jameson

We find a delight in
the beauty and
happiness of children
that makes the heart
too big for the body.

Ralph Waldo Emerson

Happiness is waking to a
sunny day and feeling that
golden-honey sensation
on my skin.

Sarah Stacey

Storybook happiness involves every form of pleasant thumb-twiddling; true happiness involves the full use of one's powers and talents.

Johann Wolfgang von Goethe

There is nothing which has yet been contrived by man, by which so much happiness is produced as by a good tavern or inn.

Samuel Johnson

It is happiness and comfort
for us men to have a
precious sweetheart.

Martin Bormann

When we recall the past,
we usually find that it is the
simplest things—not the
great occasions—that in
retrospect give off the
greatest glow of happiness.

Bob Hope

Derive happiness in oneself
from a good day's work.

Henri Matisse

Happiness is a
warm puppy.

Charles M. Schulz

Life's truest happiness is found in friendships we make along the way.

Author unknown

Out in the snow we are all young again, glowing with the happiness of childhood, and the heady sense that the world is reborn.

Libby Purves

A home-baked,
hot-buttered bun
simply oozes
happiness.

Catriona Howatson

Happiness is a butterfly which when pursued is always beyond our grasp, but which if you will sit down quietly may alight upon you.

Nathaniel Hawthorne

Picture Credits

Cover: Cuddly Kitty, 1955. © Lambert/Getty Images. p.5: Apricot Bounty, 1964. p.6: Snow Man, circa 1955, © Camerique/Getty Images. p.9: Tree Swing, circa 1925, © Lambert/Getty Images. p.10: Tommy Steele Fans, 1957. p.13: As cover. p.14: Salty Tales, 1934. p.17: Birthday Girl, 1954. p.18: Donkey Delight, 1937. p.20: Pillow Fight, circa 1950. p.23: Golfing Buddies, circa 1955, © Lambert/Getty Images. p.25: Puppies, 1936. p.26: Permanent Wave, 1954. p.29: Cider Buffs, 1935. p.30: Gee Up, 1935. p.32: Friends, 1940. p.35: Soda Smile, circa 1955, © Lambert/Getty Images. p.36: Train Of Thought, 1957. p.39: Reading In Library, 1962. p.40: Hula Family, circa 1955. p.43: Elderly Reader, 1944. p.44: Chimps' Football, 1963. p.47: Marital Bliss, circa 1965, © Lambert/Getty Images. p.49: Spoilt For Choice, 1935. p.50: Happy Cooks, 1959. p.53: Knitting Club, 1938. p.54: Spinning Around, circa 1955, © Lambert/Getty Images. p.57: Outdoor Cooking, circa 1965, © Lambert/Getty Images. p.58: Horse Lover, circa 1970. p.61: Street Cricket, 1939. p.62: Roller Girls, circa 1955, © Lambert/Getty Images. p.64: Row Your Boat, circa 1945, © Lambert/Getty Images. p.67: Pastries And Coffee, circa 1955. p.68: Pirate Scarecrow, circa 1955, © Lambert/Getty Images. p.71: Laughing Girl, 1945. p.72: Art Mirrors Life, circa 1935. p.75: Bath Time, 1951. p.76: Fishing With Sticks, circa 1945, © Lambert/Getty Images. p.79: Stack 'Em High, 1964. p.81: Leg Massage, 1939. p.82: On Santa's Knee, circa 1935, © Camerique/Getty Images. p.85: Bottoms Up, 1936. p.87: Seaside Show, 1952. p.88: Sun Worshipping, circa 1955. p.91: Lazy Sunday Afternoon, circa 1945, © Lambert/Getty Images. p.92: Crowded Bar, 1939. p.95: First Love, 1965. p.96: Octogenarian, 1936. p.99: Tiddler Season, 1936. p.101: Puppy Love, circa 1955. p.103: Happy Hikers, 1955. p.104: Home-Made Sledge, 1941. p.107: Hot Cross Buns, 1937. p.108: Village Green Match, 1966.

Text Credits

Published by MQ Publications Limited

12 The Ivories, 6–8 Northampton Street, London, N1 2HY

Tel: + 44 (0)20 7359 2244   Fax: + 44 (0)20 7359 1616

e-mail: mail@mqpublications.com

website: www.mqpublications.com

ISBN: 1-84072-479-X

1 3 5 7 9 0 8 6 4 2

Text compilation: Libby Willis

Printed and bound in China